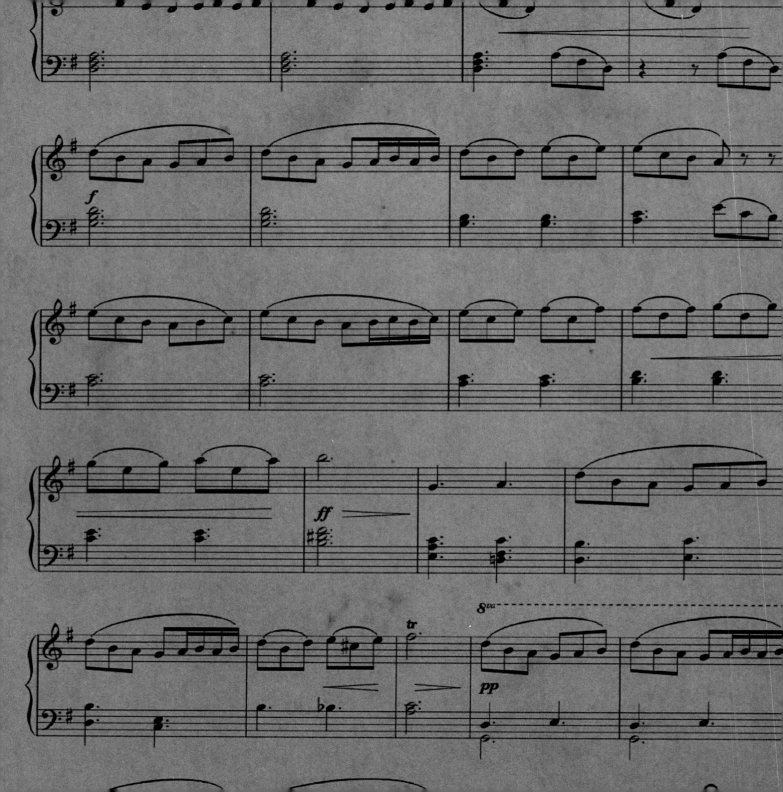

Do Superheroes Play the Piano?

by Denise Shick

Illustrated by Yana Popova

Lucas and Ricky are friends. They play superheroes together after school.

One day, when they were playing in the backyard, Lucas heard music coming from an open window in Ricky's house.

What's *that*? Lucas asked.

"That's Allison," Ricky said, "my big sister. She plays the piano every day."

He placed his hands over his ears. "I get tired of listening to the same song over and over."

Lucas thought the sound was beautiful.

"I wish I had a sister who played the piano. I like music."

From then on, Lucas looked forward to hearing Allison's music.

Several weeks later on his way to Ricky's bedroom, Lucas passed the room where Allison was playing the piano. He walked in and stood near her.

She stopped playing. "Hello, Lucas."

"I like your music," he said.

Allison smiled. "Playing the piano makes me happy."

"Is it fun?"

"I think so." She motioned for him to come closer.

"Here. Put your fingers on the keyboard and press down."
Lucas played a few notes, then someone stomped into the room.

"What are you doing?" Ricky shouted.

Lucas pulled his hands away from the piano, stepped back, and
turned around. He stuffed his hands in his pockets to keep them
from shaking.

Ricky's face was red. "Boys don't play the piano. That's girl stuff." He motioned with his hand. "Come on, Lucas. Let's play superheroes."

Lucas followed Ricky out into the hallway. He rubbed his fingers against one another, remembering the smoothness of the piano keys and the beautiful sound they made.

That night at dinner, Lucas pushed his chicken nuggets around his plate with his fork.

"What's wrong, Lucas?" Mom asked. "Aren't you hungry?"

"Ricky's sister Allison plays the piano. I like the way it sounds."

"I like piano music too," Mom said.

"Ricky says piano is for girls."

"That's not true," Dad said. "Lots of boys play the piano. I took piano lessons when I was your age."

"You did?"

"Yeah. Uncle Charlie and I both did."

"Why don't you play the piano now?" Lucas asked.

Dad shrugged. "I got interested in video games and computers." He looked over at Mom and wiggled his eyebrows. "And girls."

Mom laughed. "But your brother still plays piano in the community jazz band, right, honey?"

"Yeah, he does." Dad drummed his fingers on the table, then looked over at Lucas. "I'll check with your Uncle Charlie—see when his band is going to play again. Maybe one weekend we'll drive to his house, do some fishing with him, and listen to his band."

Lucas nodded, stabbed a nugget with his fork, and chewed. After he took a drink of water, he asked, "Could I take piano lessons?"

Mom and Dad looked at each other, their eyebrows raised. Then Dad said, "Your mom and I will talk about it."

A few days later, Mom picked up Lucas from school. When he got in the car, he asked, "Why didn't I ride the school bus home?"

"I talked to Ricky's mom about Allison's piano teacher, Ms. Armstrong. We're going to see her today. She'll let us know if you're ready to take piano lessons."

When they left Ms. Armstrong's house, Lucas jumped in the air several times and waved his arms in circles as he ran to car.

She had given him a *piano book* for beginners and shown him the notes to practice.

Mom and Dad bought Lucas a small keyboard, and they set it up in his bedroom. He ran his fingers along the shiny white and black keys. "Someday," Dad said, "if you continue to practice, we'll buy you a big piano like Allison's."

A few days later Ricky came over. Lucas showed him the keyboard.

"I'm taking piano lessons," he said.

Ricky frowned. "Pianos are for girls," he said. "Are you gonna start wearing dresses too?" He shook his head. "You're a weirdo," he said, then turned and walked toward the hallway.

"I'm going to Bobby's house to play superheroes."

The door slammed behind him.

Lucas felt like someone had placed ten heavy rocks on his chest. He wanted to cry, but somehow he felt like boys weren't supposed to do that either.

At dinner that night, Dad asked, "Did you play your keyboard today?"

Lucas pushed peas into the mashed potatoes on his plate and buried them. "No."

"Why not?"

Lucas looked up at Dad, then over at Mom. The tears spilled out before he could stop them. His face grew hot. He pushed away from the table, ran upstairs to his room, and shut the door with a bang.

A few minutes later, someone knocked on his bedroom door. "Lucas," Dad said, "May I come in?"

"Okay."

Dad sat next to him on the bed. "What happened today, son? Why didn't you play your keyboard?"

Lucas stared at the superhero poster on his wall.

"You can tell me anything." Dad placed his hand on Lucas's knee and patted it.

"Ricky said pianos are for girls. He said I should wear dresses too. He called me a weirdo." His throat felt tight as he squeezed out the words. "Ricky doesn't want to play with me anymore. He went to Bobby's house."

Lucas wiped the tears off his cheeks and looked up at Dad. "What if I don't want to play superheroes all the time like Ricky? Playing music makes me happy too." More tears slid out. "What's wrong with me? Why do I like girl stuff?"

Dad put his arm around Lucas's shoulders and pulled him close. "Nothing's wrong with you. I think it's wonderful that you like music. So does Mom." They sat quiet.

Lucas felt some of his sadness slip away.

Then Dad said, "Is it okay if I show you something in your Bible?"

Lucas nodded.

Dad stood and walked over to the desk. He picked up Lucas's Bible and brought it back to the bed. He flipped through the pages until he found the picture of David and the giant, Goliath. "David didn't have super powers, did he, son?"

Lucas shook his head.

"But he was smart and brave enough to use his skill with a slingshot. He trusted God to help him defeat Goliath. He was a hero, wasn't he?"

"Yeah." He wondered why was Dad talking about David and Goliath.

"I want you to know something else about David." Dad flipped a few pages and showed Lucas another picture, one of David playing a musical instrument. He pointed to the instrument. "That's a harp. David loved music. He wrote songs and played them."

He smoothed Lucas's hair with his hand. "God gave David many skills. He was a brave soldier who became a smart king. He was also a very good harp player."

When Dad stopped talking, Lucas looked up at him. "You can be both, son. You can be as brave as a superhero and you can love music."

Lucas studied the pattern of the rug while Dad's words swirled in his brain, then settled in his heart. He could be both.

"And you know what?" Dad set aside the book and turned to face Lucas.

"What?"

"When I hear someone play a beautiful song in church, I'm sorry I stopped taking piano lessons." He tapped Lucas's nose. "Don't give up."

Dad walked to the door, then turned around. "I'll call Uncle Charlie now. See when we can visit, okay?"

Lucas nodded. "Sure, Dad, that'll be fun." He slid off the bed and walked over to his keyboard.

The next afternoon, Lucas took his Bible over to Ricky's house. When Ricky answered the door, Lucas said, "I want to show you something."

They went to Ricky's room. Lucas showed him the pictures of David and told him the stories. "David was a brave hero and he liked music. Boys can be both. I can be both."

Ricky took the Bible from Lucas's hands and set it on his lap. He flipped back and forth between the pages, studying the pictures.

"And you know what else?" Lucas said. "My dad used to play piano and my Uncle Charlie still does."

Ricky looked at Lucas and smiled. "Some heroes play music."

"Boys can do both." Lucas stood.
"Come on, let's play superheroes."

THE END

Endorsements

Do Superheroes Play the Piano? tells the tale of Lucas as he painfully learns that there are many ways to be a boy. A boy is a boy, regardless of interests, talents, size, looks, mannerisms, and come what may. Sex is determined at conception, when science shows life begins, and Lucas's sex is stamped on every one of his cells having a nucleus. A boy is a boy."

—Andre Van Mol, MD
Board-certified Family Physician
Co-chair, Committee on Adolescent Sexuality, American College of Pediatricians
Co-chair, Sexual and Gender Identity Task Force, Christian Medical & Dental Assoc.

"Denise Shick wrote *Do Superheroes Play Piano?* as both a delightful storybook for children and a Bible-based instructional manual for parents. This book provides parents with a non-threatening way, through story telling, to approach topics like gender identity, faith, childhood teasing, and problem solving. I can confidently recommend this book to families."

—Sheri Golden, PhD
Licensed Professional Counselor

"After I read *Do Superheroes Play the Piano?* I thought, Wow! This is great! As the grandfather of five beautiful gifts from God, I want each of them to read this book and celebrate their God-given skills and interests. This has everything you want in a children's book, or any book for that matter. It is well-written, age appropriate, and delivers an important message not only for children but for every person. That is a powerful trifecta for highly recommending Denise Shick's book. I can't wait to get my copy for my grandkids!"

—Dr. James M. Reeves, Senior Pastor, City on a Hill Church
Producer, Director of The Fearless Series for Women
FS4Women.com

For Parents:

If you want to read more about David, some of his story is told in the book of 1 Samuel, chapters 16–18.

If your son struggles with his identity as a boy, here are some Scripture passages that may help him understand that God gives different skills and interests to each boy and that all of them can be used to serve God.

Psalm 139:14–16 affirms that God designed every part of him—both his appearance and interests.

Jeremiah 1:5 affirms that God has a purpose for him and has given him the interests and abilities he needs to become the boy God designed him to be.

Exodus 28:3–4 describes the skilled clothes designers and weavers God used to make fancy clothing for the priests. These men were just as valuable to God as the warriors and farmers.

Exodus 31:1–11 introduces Bezalel, Oholiab, and other craftsman who were filled with the Spirit of God and able to create all kinds of beautiful objects—furniture, jewelry, bowls, and fabrics. They were just as valuable to God as warriors and farmers. (Also see Exodus 35:30–35, 36:8, and 37:29).

First Samuel 16:18 describes David as a young man who was both a warrior and a musician. Many of the songs he wrote are in the book of Psalms, including Psalm 8 and Psalm 23.

Second Samuel 6:14–15 records that David, and many others, danced before the Lord as an act of worship.

First Chronicles 15:16–19 lists some of the hundreds of singers and musicians David appointed to lead worship. Also see 2 Chronicles 5:11–12.

Do Superheroes Play the Piano?

ISBN: 978-1-7365951-6-9

9 781736 595169

Made in the USA
Columbia, SC
22 March 2023

14158114R00020